THIS IS MY
NEW YORK

BIS

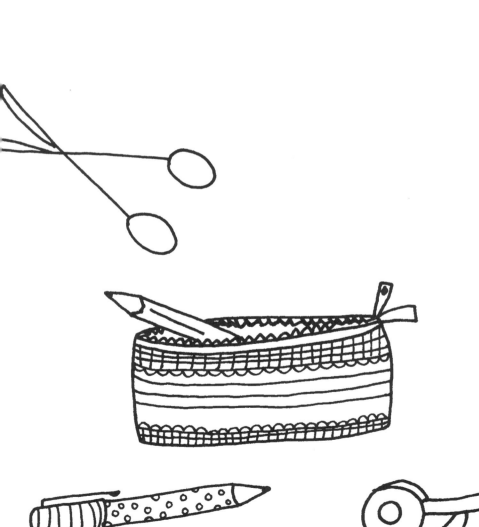

THIS BOOK BELONGS TO

DATE

THESE STREETS WILL MAKE YOU

WILL INSPIRE YOU, LET'S HEAR

-ALICIA KEYS FT JAY-Z

FEEL BRAND NEW, THE LIGHTS

FOR NEW YORK!

Things I would like to see and do in New York

MARKERS, PENS, PENCILS & TUBES OF PAINT

BLICK
536 Myrtle Avenue
Brooklyn, NY 11205-2606

THE INK PAD
37 Seventh Avenue
(Corner of 13th Street)
New York City, NY 10011

SOHO ART MATERIALS
7 Wooster Street
New York City, NY 10013

NEW YORK CENTRAL
62 Third Avenue
New York City, NY 10003

UTRECHT ART SUPPLIES
21 East 13th Street
New York City, NY 10003

DA VINCI ARTIST SUPPLY
170 East 70th Street
New York City, NY 10021

ARTIST & CRAFTSMAN SUPPLY
761 Metropolitan Avenue
Brooklyn, NY 11211

SUBWAY FOR PROS

Draw from the example of an actual subway map: which subway have you taken, where did you get off, and what are the most beautiful names?

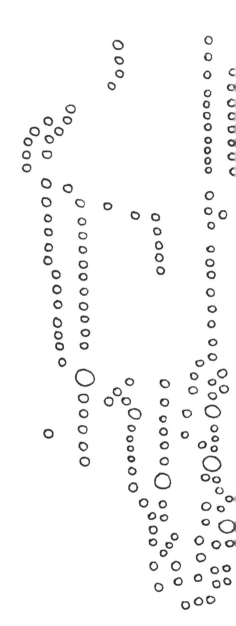

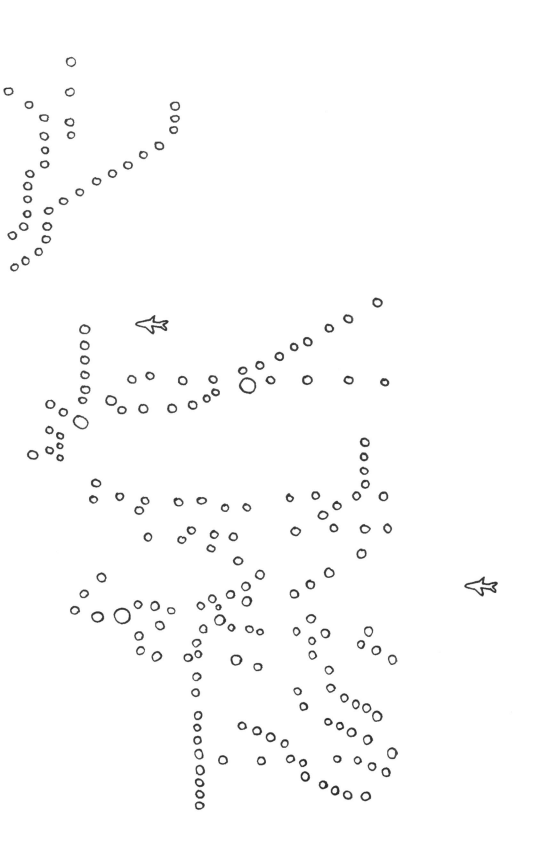

DOUBLE ESPRESSO & FLAT WHITE: THE VERY BEST COFFEE IN NYC *

☐ **LA COLOMBE**
400 Lafayette Street
New York City, NY 10003

☐ **HAPPY BONES**
394 Broome Street
New York City, NY 10013

☐ **TOBY'S ESTATE COFFEE**
125 North 6th Street
Brooklyn, NY 11249

☐ **CAFÉ GRUMPY**
193 Meserole Avenue
Brooklyn, NY 11222

☐ **EVERYMAN ESPRESSO**
301 West Broadway
New York City, NY 10013

☐ **STUMPTOWN COFFEE ROASTERS**
30 West 8th Street
New York City, NY 10011

☐ **BLUE BOTTLE COFFEE**
450 West 15th Street
New York City, NY 10014

☐ **NINTH STREET ESPRESSO**
341 East 10th Street
New York City, NY 10009

☐ **JOE COFFEE**
405 West 23rd Street
New York City, NY 10011

☐ **SWEETLEAF**
10-93 Jackson Avenue
Long Island City, NY 11101

☐ ....

☐ ....

☐ ....

☐ ....

☐ ....

☐ ....

* Most of these venues can found at multiple
locations in the city, as well as throughout the USA.

TICKETS & BUSINESS CARDS

Add your most beautiful ones to this page, or copy them in a drawing.

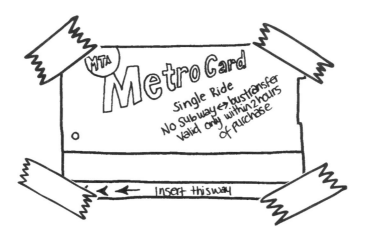

STATEN ISLAND FERRY

Large, bright yellow boats
– each one slightly different –
offer free daily transport between
Manhattan and Staten Island to
thousands of New Yorkers.
Even for non-commuters it is fun
to go for a trip on the ferry, as it
offers you a splendid view of the
city.

TO GO OR
NOT TO GO

Truly, you can find incredibly delicious coffee in the USA – at the beginning of this book, a few addresses for finding a good *cup of joe* are suggested. Ten times better than most road movies will have you believe (diners with coffee that has been simmering on a hot plate for hours, no thanks). You will not mind being seen with one of these to-go cups!

SIGHTS YOU WILL NOT WANT TO MISS

You do not need to visit them – as doing nothing in a city can also be really satisfying – but these highlights are widely beloved for a reason.
Tick off the places you have visited.

- ☐ EMPIRE STATE BUILDING
- ☐ STATUE OF LIBERTY
- ☐ ELLIS ISLAND
- ☐ HIGH LINE
- ☐ CHRYSLER BUILDING
- ☐ BROOKLYN BRIDGE
- ☐ TIMES SQUARE
- ☐ CENTRAL PARK
- ☐ FIFTH AVENUE
- ☐ BROADWAY
- ☐ GROUND ZERO
- ☐ FLATIRON BUILDING
- ☐ HUDSON RIVER PARK
- ☐ BATTERY PARK
- ☐ ONE WORLD OBSERVATORY
- ☐ BROOKLYN HEIGHTS PROMENADE
- ☐ FORT WADSWORTH
- ☐ ....
- ☐ ....
- ☐ ....

CHOCOLATE CHIP COOKIES

Coffee with something sweet; the options in NYC are endless. These cookies can be found all across the city and are easily made in no time at all.

175 gr. butter, melted 125 gr.
(light brown) sugar
1 egg
250 gr. flour
½ tsp. baking powder
knife tip of salt
100 gr. cooking chocolate (drops)
EXTRA baking tray covered with baking paper

Mix the melted butter and the sugar until the sugar has dissolved as much as possible and then whisk in the egg. In another bowl mix the flour, baking powder and salt. Add the butter mixture, stir it well and then stir in most of the chocolate drops (but keep a few for garnish). Place the dough in the fridge for 1 hour.

Preheat the oven at 175°C. Make balls the size of a golf ball and place them on the baking tray with ample space between them. Bake the cookies 10-15 minutes; they should not be baked too crispy. A decent cookie is crisp, but also a bit soggy. Repeat with the rest of the dough.

BETHESDA FOUNTAIN

The largest fountain in all of New York can be found in the middle of Central Park.

Naturally, it is a bit cheesy, but very many tourists want to take their picture with this fountain at all costs. This also goes for celebrating special occasions: countless wedding shoots have been held here.

The fountain was placed to commemorate the moment at which clean drinking water was available in the city for the first time, in the year 1842.

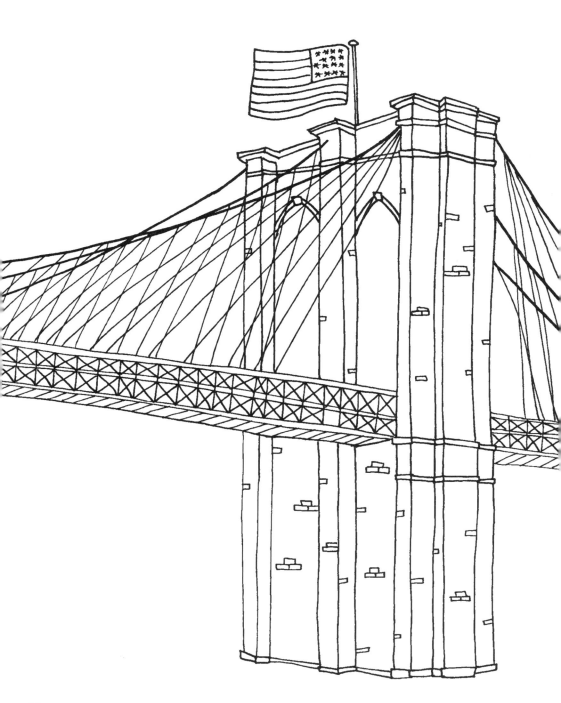

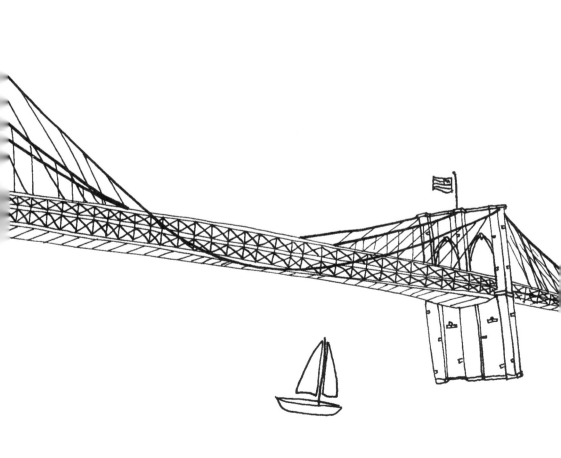

TIME FOR A DRINK!

Yes, there are bars enough in the city, but if you want to do something special, then you might want to look out for a rooftop terrace. Drink a cocktail and enjoy the breath-taking view over the city. Especially during sunset, of course.

42 ISLANDS,
5 BOROUGHS,
68 NEIGHBORHOODS

In what neighbourhood did you stay or where would you love to have an apartment? The five boroughs Manhattan, The Bronx, Brooklyn, Queens and Staten Island are subdivided into 68 smaller districts, the neighbourhoods. The city has many small islands, most of which are uninhabited. In case of a flood, some even fully disappear under water!

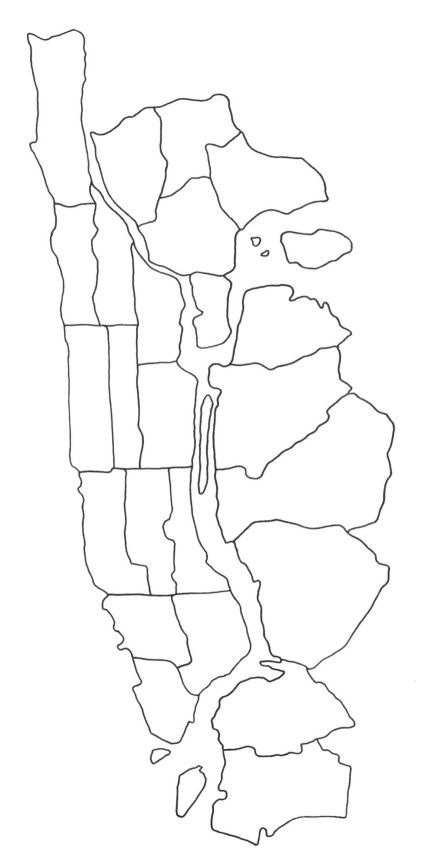

Dreams, notes, ideas, inventions

THE MOST BEAUTIFUL MUSEUMS

There are hundreds of museums in New York – and that's not even including the galleries. In any case, these 11 are well worth your while.

THE 4 MOST FAMOUS ONES

☐ METROPOLITAN MUSEUM OF ART (THE MET)
www.metmuseum.org

☐ MUSEUM OF MODERN ART (MOMA)
www.moma.org

☐ GUGGENHEIM
www.guggenheim.org/new-york

☐ AMERICAN MUSEUM OF NATURAL HISTORY
www.amnh.org

☐ ....

☐ ....

☐ ....

PLUS 7 EXTRAORDINARY ONES

☐ WILLIAMSBURG ART & HISTORICAL CENTER
www.wahcenter.net

☐ COOPER-HEWITT NATIONAL DESIGN MUSEUM
www.cooperhewitt.org

☐ THE JEWISH MUSEUM
www.thejewishmuseum.org

☐ MUSEUM OF ARTS AND DESIGN (MAD)
www.madmuseum.org

☐ WHITNEY MUSEUM OF AMERICAN ART
www.whitney.org

☐ INTERNATIONAL CENTRE OF PHOTOGRAPHY (ICP)
www.icp.org

☐ 9/11 MEMORIAL
www.911memorial.org

☐ ....

☐ ....

☐ ....

STATUE OF LIBERTY

No crowd of waving people can beat this: the Statue of Liberty on Liberty Island greets all newcomers to the USA.
The statue was a gift from France in commemoration of the Declaration of Independence of the USA. In 1776, The States became independent from the British monarchy. On 28 October 1885, the statue was revealed. Annually, roughly 4 million visitors flock to the statue. Of course, flying over it with a helicopter is even more spectacular.

HOT DOGS & STREET FOOD MARKETS & TRUCKS

Just like in the movies or your favourite Netflix series: buying a hot dog at one of the many stalls on the sidewalk. With sauerkraut, of course. For those who would rather enjoy a trendy sandwich someplace nice, there are many good and attractive delis in the city, but also the necessary street food markets. Not to be missed either: the many food trucks. There are too many great addresses to name, so the list on this page will also provide you with some good websites that can point you to excellent locations.

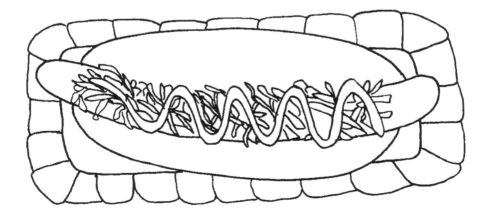

WHERE?

☐ **NYCFOODTRUCK**
nyctruckfood.com

☐ **SMORGASBURG FOOD MARKET**
www.smorgasburg.com

☐ **KATZ'S DELICATESSEN**
205 East Houston Street
New York City, NY 10002

☐ **GANSEVOORT MARKET**
52 Gansevoort Street
New York City, NY 10014

☐ **DEAN & DELUCA**
560 Broadway
New York City, NY 10012

☐ **SHAKE SHACK**
Madison Square Park
New York, NY 10010

☐ ....

WHAT?

☐ CLASSIC GRILLED CHEESE
☐ LOBSTER ROLL
☐ TACO'S
☐ REUBEN SANDWICH
☐ PASTRAMI SANDWICH
☐ SAUKERKRAUT HOT DOG
☐ BAGEL
☐ EGGS BENEDICT

☐ ....

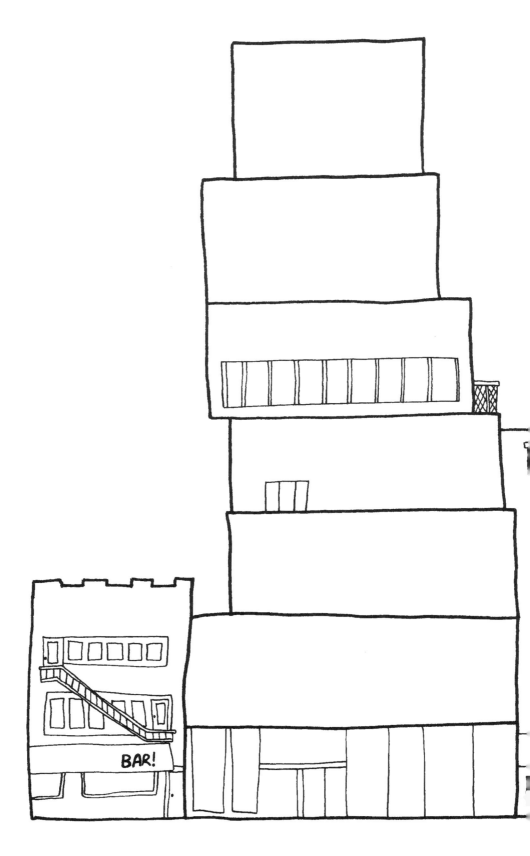

NEW MUSEUM

It looks just like a stack of shoe boxes piled messily on top of each other, but the design of the New Museum (235 Bowery, New York City, NY 10002) has – of course – carefully been thought out. You can walk around here for hours; the building offers a place full of beautiful installations and exhibitions of international artists. Definitely worth a visit if you are looking for a good dose of inspiration.

FLEA MARKETS

A nice visit to the flea market. In New York that means you will also encounter many vintage and art items. The markets below are worth your while, but you will most likely find some yourself, too.

☐ **ARTISTS & FLEAS**
70 North 7th Street
Brooklyn, NY 11249
www.artistsandfleas.com

☐ **CHELSEA FLEA MARKET**
28 West 25th Street
New York City, NY 10010
www.annexmarkets.com

☐ **HELL'S KITCHEN FLEA MARKET**
West 39th Street between 9th & 10th Avenue
New York City, NY 10018
www.annexmarkets.com

☐ **LIC FLEA & FOOD**
5-25 46th Avenue
Long Island City, NY 11101
www.licflea.com

☐ **THE MARKET NYC**
218 Bedford Avenue
Brooklyn, NY 11249
www.themarketnyc.com

☐ ....

☐ ....

☐ ....

The city, the people, the sounds, the smells

FILMS IN, ABOUT & FROM NEW YORK

☐ TAXI DRIVER

☐ KING KONG

☐ SATURDAY NIGHT FEVER

☐ ANNIE HALL

☐ BREAKFAST AT TIFFANY'S

☐ THE WOLF OF WALL STREET

☐ BLUE JASMINE

☐ EXTREMELY LOUD & INCREDIBLY CLOSE

☐ NEW YORK, I LOVE YOU

☐ JULIE & JULIA

☐ WHEN HARRY MET SALLY

☐ MAN ON WIRE

☐ THE FRENCH CONNECTION

☐ ....

☐ ....

☐ ....

NEW YORK, NEW YORK...

- [ ] FRANK SINATRA: THEME FROM NEW YORK, NEW YORK
- [ ] LEONARD COHEN: CHELSEA HOTEL NO. 2
- [ ] BRUCE SPRINGSTEEN: THE RISING
- [ ] BEASTIE BOYS: NO SLEEP TILL BROOKLYN
- [ ] BILLIE HOLIDAY: AUTUMN IN NEW YORK
- [ ] LOU REED: WALK ON THE WILD SIDE
- [ ] JAY Z & ALICIA KEYS: EMPIRE STATE OF MIND
- [ ] THE LOVIN' SPOONFUL: SUMMER IN THE CITY
- [ ] BOBBY WOMACK & PEACE: ACROSS 110TH STREET
- [ ] ....
- [ ] ....
- [ ] ....

CONEY ISLAND LUNA PARK

The fun parks and Coney Island, a peninsula in the south of Brooklyn, have become synonymous. There can never be too many of this type of beautiful gateways, faded glory or not. This gateway is that of Luna Park, which was opened in 1903 and still attracts many visitors.

PLEASE DO NOT SMILE AT STRANGERS

At which stops did you get off? Tick them off here!

1st Avenue
2nd Avenue
3rd Avenue
3rd Avenue-138th Street
3rd Avenue-149th Street
4th Avenue
5th Avenue
5th Avenue-Bryant Park
5th Avenue/53rd Street
6th Avenue
7th Avenue
8th Avenue
8th Street
9th Avenue
9th Street
14th Street
15th Street-Prospect Park
18th Avenue
18th Street
20th Avenue
21st Street
21st Street-Queensbridge
23rd Street
23rd Street-Ely Avenue
25th Avenue
25th Street
28th Street
30th Avenue-Grand Avenue
33rd Street
33rd Street-Rawson Street
34th Street-Herald Square
34th Street-Penn Station
34th Street-Penn Station
36th Avenue-Washington Avenue
36th Street
39th Avenue-Beebe Avenue
40th Street-Lowery Street
42nd Street-Bryant Park
42nd Street-Grand Central
42nd Street-Port Authority Bus Terminal
45th Road-Court House Square
45th Street
46th Street
46th Street-Bliss Street
47th-50th Streets-Rockefeller Center
49th Street
50th Street
51st Street
52nd Street-Lincoln Avenue
53rd Street
55th Street
57th Street
59th Street
59th Street-Columbus Circle
61st Street-Woodside
62nd Street
63rd Drive-Rego Park
65th Street

66th Street-Lincoln Center
67th Avenue
68th Street-Hunter College
69th Street-Fisk Avenue
71st Street
72nd Street
74th Street-Broadway
75th Avenue
75th Street
77th Street
79th Street
80th Street-Hudson Street
81st Street-Museum of Natural History
82nd Street-Jackson Heights
85th Street-Forest Parkway
86th Street
88th Street-Boyd Avenue
90th Street-Elmhurst Avenue
95th Street
96th Street
103rd Street
103rd Street-Corona Plaza
104th Street
110th Street
110th Street-Central Park North
111th Street
116th Street
116th Street-Columbia University
121st Street
125th Street
135th Street
137th Street-City College
138th Street
145th Street
148th Street-Lenox Terminal
149th Street-Grand Concourse
14th Street-Union Square
155th Street
157th Street
161st Street
161st Street-Yankee Stadium
163rd Street
167th Street
168th Street
169th Street
170th Street
174th Street
174th-175th Streets
175th Street-GW Bridge Bus Terminal
176th Street
179th Street
181st Street
182nd-183rd Streets
183rd Street
190th Street
191st Street
205th Street

207th Street
215th Street
219th Street
225th Street
231st Street
233rd Street
238th Street
241st Street
Alabama Avenue
Allerton Avenue
Aqueduct Racetrack
Aqueduct-North Conduit Avenue
Astor Place
Astoria Boulevard
Atlantic Avenue
Atlantic Avenue-Pacific Street
Avenue H
Avenue I
Avenue J
Avenue M
Avenue N
Avenue P
Avenue U
Avenue X
Bay 50th Street
Bay Parkway
Bay Ridge Avenue
Baychester Avenue
Beach 105th Street-Seaside
Beach 25th Street-Wavecrest
Beach 36th Street-Edgemere
Beach 44th Street-Frank Avenue
Beach 60th Street-Straiton
Beach 67th Street-Gaston
Beach 90th Street-Holland
Beach 98th Street-Playland
Bedford Avenue
Bedford Park Boulevard
Bedford-Nostrand Avenues
Bergen Street
Beverley Road
Beverly Road
Bleecker Street
Borough Hall
Botanic Garden
Bowery
Bowling Green
Briarwood-Van Wyck
Brighton Beach
Broad Channel
Broad Street
Broadway
Broadway Junction
Broadway-Lafayette Street
Broadway-Nassau Street
Bronx Park East
Brook Avenue
Brooklyn Bridge-City Hall
Buhre Avenue

Burke Avenue
Burnside Avenue
Bushwick Avenue-Aberdeen Street
Canal Street
Carroll Street
Castle Hill Avenue
Cathedral Parkway-110th Street
Central Avenue
Chambers Street
Chauncey Street
Christopher Street
Church Avenue
City Hall
Clark Street
Classon Avenue
Cleveland Street
Clinton-Washington Avenues
Coney Island-Stillwell Avenue
Cortelyou Road
Cortlandt Street
Court Square
Court Street
Crescent Street
Cypress Avenue
Cypress Hills
Dean Street
DeKalb Avenue
Delancey Street
Ditmars Boulevard-Astoria
Ditmas Avenue
Dyckman Street
East 105th Street
East 143rd Street-St. Mary's Street
East 149th Street
East 180th Street
East 180th Street
East Broadway
Eastchester-Dyre Avenue
Eastern Parkway-Brooklyn Museum
Elder Avenue
Elmhurst Avenue
Essex Street
Euclid Avenue
Far Rockaway-Mott Avenue
Flatbush Avenue
Flushing Avenue
Fordham Road
Forest Avenue
Forest Hills-71st Avenue
Fort Hamilton Parkway
Franklin Avenue
Franklin Street
Freeman Street
Fresh Pond Road
Fulton Street
Gates Avenue

Graham Avenue
Grand Army Plaza
Grand Avenue-Newtown
Grand Street
Grant Avenue
Greenpoint Avenue
Gun Hill Road
Halsey Street
Hewes Street
High Street-Brooklyn Bridge
Howard Beach-JFK
Hoyt Street-Fulton Mall
Hoyt-Schermerhorn Street
Hunters Point Avenue
Hunts Point Avenue
Intervale Avenue
Jackson Avenue
Jamaica Center-Parsons/
Archer
Jamaica-Van Wyck
Jay Street-Borough Hall
Jefferson Street
Junction Boulevard
Junius Street
Kings Highway
Kingsbridge Road
Kingston Avenue
Kingston-Throop Avenues
Knickerbocker Avenue
Kosciuszko Street
Lafayette Avenue
Lawrence Street-MetroTech
Lefferts Boulevard
Lexington Avenue-53rd Street
Lexington Avenue-63rd Street
Lexington Avenue/59th Street
Liberty Avenue
Livonia Avenue
Longwood Avenue
Lorimer Street
Main Street-Flushing
Marble Hill-225th Street
Marcy Avenue
Metropolitan Avenue
Middletown Road
Montrose Avenue
Morgan Avenue
Morris Park
Morrison-Sound View
Avenues
Mosholu Parkway
Mount Eden Avenue
Myrtle Avenue
Myrtle-Willoughby Avenues
Myrtle-Wyckoff Avenues
Nassau Avenue
Neck Road
Neptune Avenue
Nereid Avenue
Nevins Street
New Lots Avenue
New Utrecht Avenue
Newkirk Avenue
Northern Boulevard
Norwood Avenue
Nostrand Avenue
Ocean Parkway
Park Place
Parkchester

Parkside Avenue
Parsons Boulevard
Pelham Bay Park
Pelham Parkway
Pennsylvania Avenue
President Street
Prince Street
Prospect Avenue
Prospect Park
Queens Plaza
Queensboro Plaza
Ralph Avenue
Rector Street
Rockaway Avenue
Rockaway Boulevard
Rockaway Park-Beach 116th
Street
Rockaway Parkway
Roosevelt Avenue-Jackson
Heights
Roosevelt Island
Saratoga Avenue
Seneca Avenue
Sheepshead Bay
Shepherd Avenue
Simpson Street
Smith-Ninth Streets
South Ferry
Spring Street
St. Lawrence Avenue
Steinway Street
Sterling Street
Sutphin Boulevard
Sutphin Boulevard-Archer
Avenue-JFK
Sutter Avenue
Sutter Avenue-Rutland Road
Times Square
Times Square-42nd Street
Tremont Avenue
Union Square-14th Street
Union Street
Union Turnpike-Kew Gardens
Utica Avenue
Van Cortlandt Park-242nd
Street
Van Siclen Avenue
Vernon Boulevard-Jackson
Avenue
Wall Street
West Eighth Street-New York
Aquarium
West Farms Square-East
Tremont Avenue
West Fourth Street-Washing-
ton Square
Westchester Square-East
Tremont Avenue
Whitehall Street-South Ferry
Whitlock Avenue
Willets Point-Shea Stadium
Wilson Avenue
Winthrop Street
Woodhaven Boulevard
Woodlawn
World Trade Center
Worth Street
York Street
Zerega Avenue

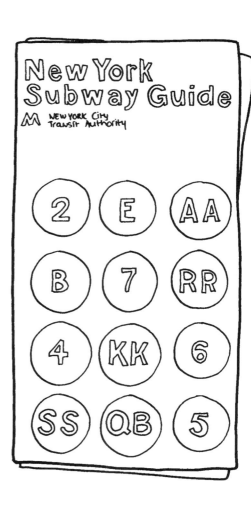

1001 SQUIRRELS

Squirrels in Central Park: adorable or not so much? You can judge for yourself. They truly live in the wild, so it is not exactly acceptable to take one home with you.

TODAY WE DO NOTHING!

Or rather, we will be relaxing and enjoying the green surroundings of High Line Park in Manhattan. In 2009, this unique project was established on the tracks of a flyover railway that hadn't been used for years.

MUSICAL, THEATRE & OPERA

To Broadway, of course. Or take the alternative route and visit a
theatre in another part of town. New York has countless theatres, so
selecting the nicest is tricky. Nevertheless, below we offer some
suggestions. If you feel like an evening of entertainment, then also
take a look at *www.newyorkcitytheatre.com*.

☐ **THE APOLLO THEATER**
253 West 125th Street
New York City, NY 10027
www.apollotheater.org

☐ **CARNEGIE HALL**
881 7th Avenue
New York City, NY 10019
www.carnegiehall.org

☐ **METROPOLITAN OPERA**
Lincoln Center for the Performing Arts
30 Lincoln Center Plaza
New York City, NY 10023
www.metopera.org

☐ **RADIO CITY MUSIC HALL**
1260 Avenue of the Americas
New York City, NY 10020
www.radiocity.com

☐ **MADISON SQUARE GARDEN CENTER**
4 Pennsylvania Plaza
New York City, NY 10001
www.thegarden.com

☐ **NEW AMSTERDAM THEATRE**
214 West 42nd Street
New York, NY 10036
www.newamsterdamtheatre.net

Spots I have visited and wish to remember

NEW YORK STOCK EXCHANGE

Perhaps the largest flag in the whole of the USA hangs from the facade of this stock exchange on Wall Street. Since 9/11, you can no longer enter as a visitor. Not far down the road, you will find a giant bronze bull by the Italian artist Arturo Di Modica. The bull was placed in front of the stock exchange in 1989, as a surprise for the New Yorkers. It actually had to be removed, but now stands – much to the satisfaction of the residents in the vicinity, who do not wish to miss their bull – in Bowling Green Park.

MAST BROTHERS CHOCOLATE

So unforgettably delicious; chocolate by the Mast Brothers (yes, they are actually two brothers). Do yourself a favour and buy a few of these slabs of chocolate. They have two shops in Williamsburg, Brooklyn, but sell their chocolate all over the world.

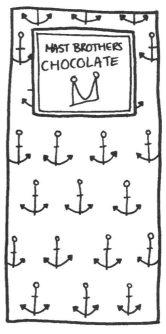

A BAD DAY IN NEW YORK CITY IS STILL BETTER THAN A GOOD DAY ANYWHERE ELSE.

JOGGERS, RUNNERS & HIKERS

Even if you do not intend to run the New York marathon: always, always, always bring a pair of running shoes in your bag when you go to NYC. Or buy nice new ones here.

BEAUTIFUL BOOKSHOPS

☐ **STRAND BOOKSTORE**
828 Broadway
Manhattan, NY 10003-4805

☐ **WORD BROOKLYN**
126 Franklin Street
Brooklyn, NY 11222

☐ **192 BOOKS**
Clement Clarke Moore Park
190 10th Avenue
New York City, NY 10011

☐ **RIZZOLI BOOKSTORE**
1133 Broadway
New York City, NY 10010

☐ **POSMAN BOOKS**
250 Vesey Street
New York City, NY 10281

☐ **MCNALLY JACKSON**
52 Prince Street
New York City, NY 10012

☐ **FORBIDDEN PLANET (COMICS)**
832 Broadway
New York City, NY 10003

☐ **GREENLIGHT**
686 Fulton Street
Brooklyn, NY 11217

☐ ....

☐ ....

☐ ....

BOOKS IN, ABOUT & FROM NEW YORK

- [ ] **BRET EASTON ELLIS,** American Psycho
- [ ] **JAY MCINERNEY,** Bright Lights, Big City
- [ ] **SYLVIA PLATH,** The Bell Jar
- [ ] **RALPH ELLISON,** Invisible Man
- [ ] **J.D. SALINGER,** The Catcher in the Rye
- [ ] **TOM WOLFE,** The Bonfire of the Vanities
- [ ] **JULIA ROTHMAN,** Hello New York
- [ ] **JAMES BALDWIN,** Another Country
- [ ] **DON DELILLO,** Underworld
- [ ] **JONATHAN SAFRAN FOER,** Extremely Loud & Incredibly Close
- [ ] **PAUL AUSTER,** The New York Trilogy
- [ ] **JEAN KWOK,** Girl in Translation
- [ ] **DONNA TARTT,** The Goldfinch
- [ ] **F. SPRINGER,** Tabee, New York
- [ ] **JONATHAN LETHEM,** The Fortress of Solitude
- [ ] **F. SCOTT FITZGERALD,** The Great Gatsby
- [ ] ....
- [ ] ....

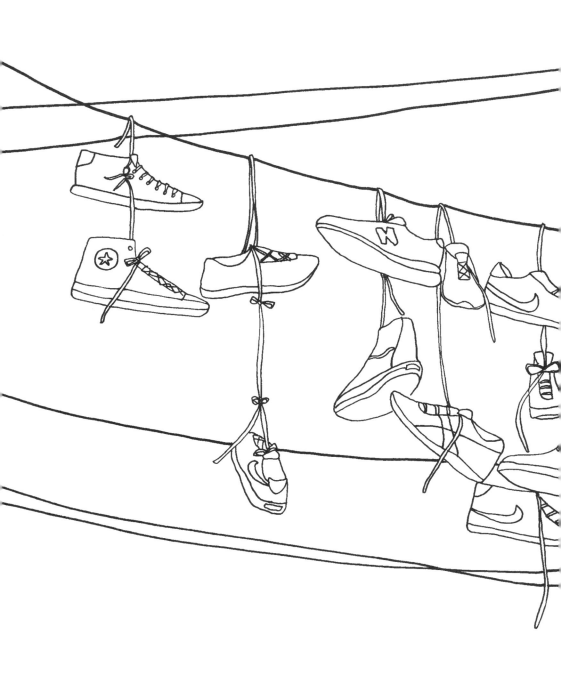

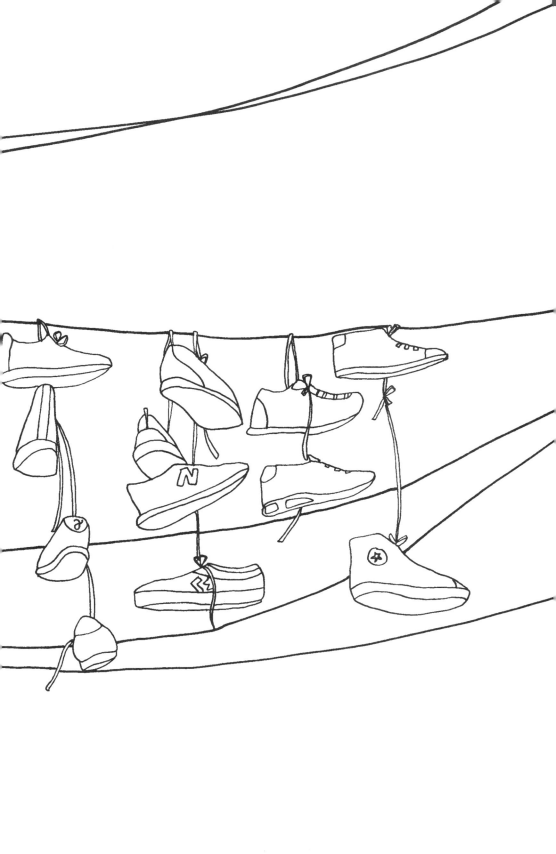

BREAKFAST
AT TIFFANY'S

This journal provides you with a
list of books that are set in New
York. One of the best-known ones
is not listed there: Breakfast at
Tiffany's by Truman Capote,
written in 1958.
The film from 1961 is perhaps even
more famous, starring Audrey
Hepburn. If it had been up to
Capote, though, Marilyn Monroe
would have played the lead role.

MAGAZINES & NEWSPAPERS

Cover junkies can really go to town here – so many beautiful magazines and newspapers are created in this city.

BETTER THAN A
TEXT MESSAGE

Below, note down the names of five people,
buy five postcards and five stamps, and then
write five beautiful sentences on each card.
Do not forget to post.

KITSCH & ART

Take a picture of the ugliest
souvenirs you encounter and
add the photographs to this page.
Or draw them. Our favourite:
the Big Apple magnet.
Or maybe rather the King Kong
mug.

WALDORF SALADE

Invented at the end of the 19th century in the famous Waldorf Astoria Hotel. The salad is delicious in all its simplicity. The quantities below are for four people.

2 tangy apples, such as Granny Smith
3 stems of celery
100 gr. of walnuts
hand of raisins or seedless red grapes
½ lemon
75 ml yoghurt
½ iceberg lettuce or 1 stalk of Roman lettuce
pepper & salt

Wash the apples and chop them in cubes or strips. Clean the celery and cut into thin arches. Mix everything in a bowl with the roughly chopped walnuts, raisins or grapes, some lemon juice and yoghurt. You can also substitute the yoghurt with mayonnaise or make a mixture of both. Cut the lettuce into strips, stir it in and add taste to the whole with some salt and pepper. Nothing to add.

MY 8 MOST BEAUTIFUL PHOTOS

Print out on 5 x 5 cm and stick
them in. Just like a real Polaroid!

BARGAINS & BAD BUYS

Regretting that one jacket you left behind? If only you could have just kept yourself from buying those expensive trousers. Draw your bad buys, bargains, and missed purchases here.

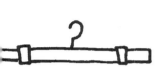 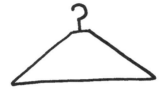 

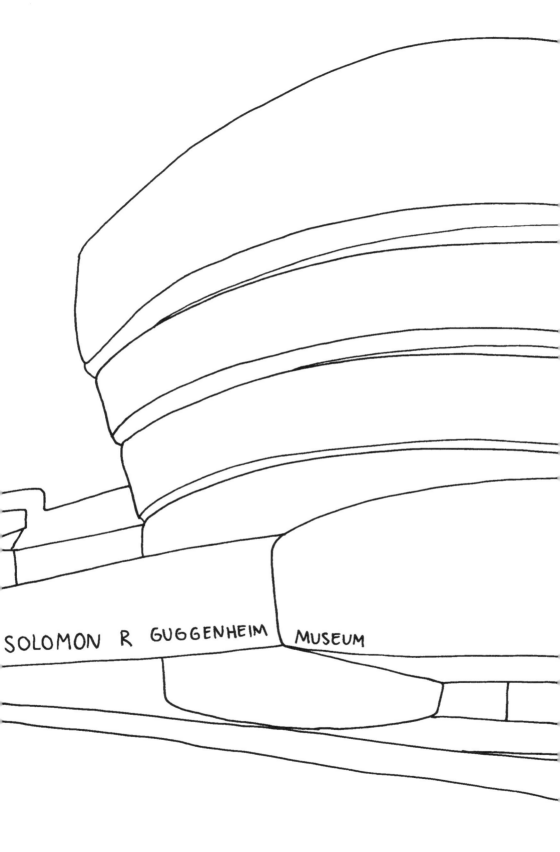

SOLOMON R GUGGENHEIM MUSEUM

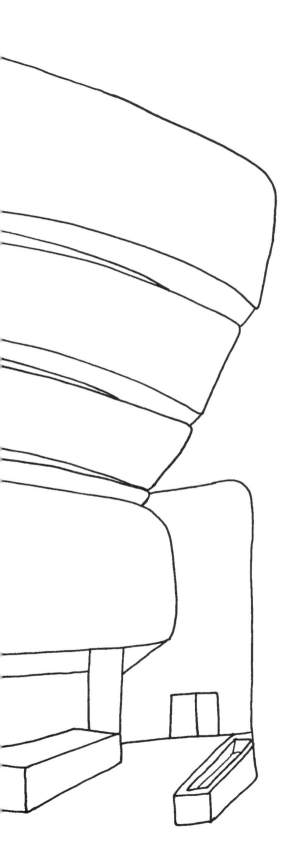

THE GUGGENHEIM

Officially, this museum – which exists since 1959 – is called the Solomon R. Guggenheim Museum, named after its founder. Its beautiful building is by the American architect Frank Lloyd Wright and poses a nightmare for many curators: it was built in the shape of a spiral and there is little light. For this very reason, it is one of the most beautiful buildings in the city.

The collection consists of modern art and is mainly in the hands of the family Guggenheim.

You will find the museum on Fifth Avenue, between 88th and 89th Street.

ROOM WITH A VIEW

Do you have a view of Central Park, a beautiful museum, or the Hudson? Is the view nice enough to copy in a drawing?

WALK & DON'T WALK

The city has almost 10 million inhabitants.
And perhaps just as many traffic signs...

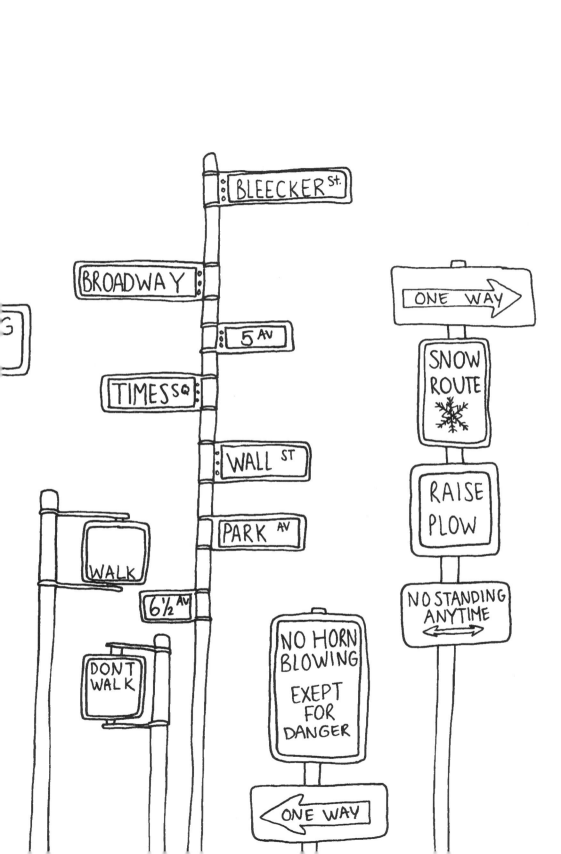

3X COCKTAIL

Delicious! Nothing beats a good cocktail. Certainly not if you are in NYC, where it is really part of the scene. Choose a rooftop terrace and enjoy. They can also easily be imitated at home, even without a bartender and tons of equipment. Pour all ingredients into a glass and taste the result.

COSMOPOLITAN

2 parts cranberry juice
2 parts vodka
1 part limen juice
1 part orange liqueur
crushed ice or ice cubes

BELLINI

½ peach, mashed
dash of Prosecco or Champagne
optional: dash of peach brandy
optional: squeeze of lemon juice
crushed ice or ice cubes

DARK 'N' STORMY

1 part rum
4 parts ginger ale
¼ lemon, segments bruised and in the glass
crushed ice or ice cubes

GRAND CENTRAL TERMINAL

The busiest train station in the USA is located in the heart of Manhattan. The station has the greatest number of platforms in the world, boasting no less than 44. The facade sports a group of statues depicting the gods Minerva, Hercules and Mercury, made by a French sculptor – this, too, is enormous. Although its exterior is already impressive, you should really step inside. The robust clock in the large hall is famous and regularly makes an appearance in TV series and films.

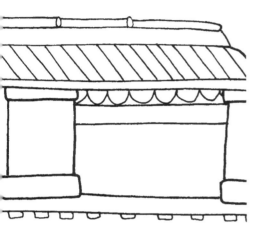

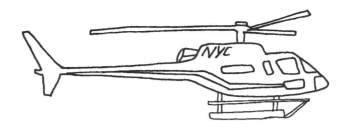

OVER THE NEW YORK ROOFTOPS

Draw the view from the Empire State Building, a rooftop terrace, or any other high vantage point in the city. Plenty to choose from!

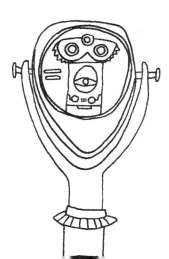

EXTREMELY LOUD & INCREDIBLY CLOSE

Americans talk louder than Europeans and the explanation for this is actually quite simple: Europeans stand nearer to each other when they speak, while Americans like to keep their distance. To ensure audibility, you then need to slightly turn up the volume. Thankfully, thinking happens in silence all over the world. This artwork by the Swiss artist Olaf Breuning with (thought) clouds used to be located in Central Park, how pretty!

Inspiration for at home, at work, on holidays, the rest of my life

TYPICAL
NEW YORK

Print out your photographs on
5 x 5 cm and glue them in here.
Just like a real Polaroid!

IN THE FUTURE EVERYBODY WILL BE WORLDFAMOUS FOR 15 MINUTES

Often spotted: restaurants displaying photographs of the owner with visiting celebrities on the wall. Also want to see such a wall? Or have you spotted a celebrity yourself?

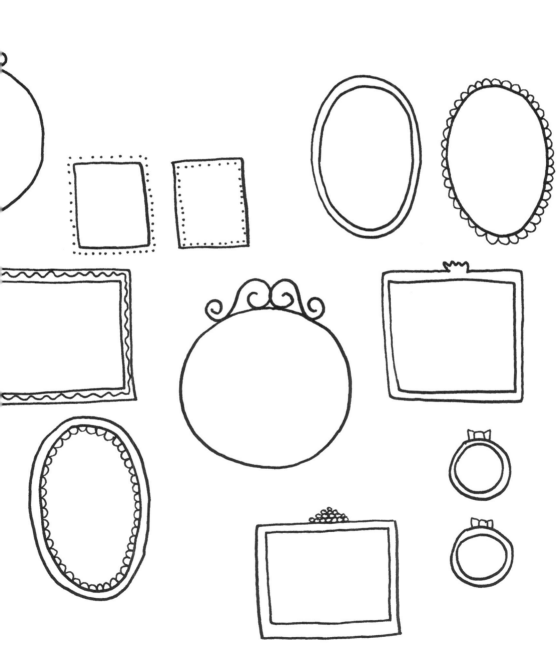

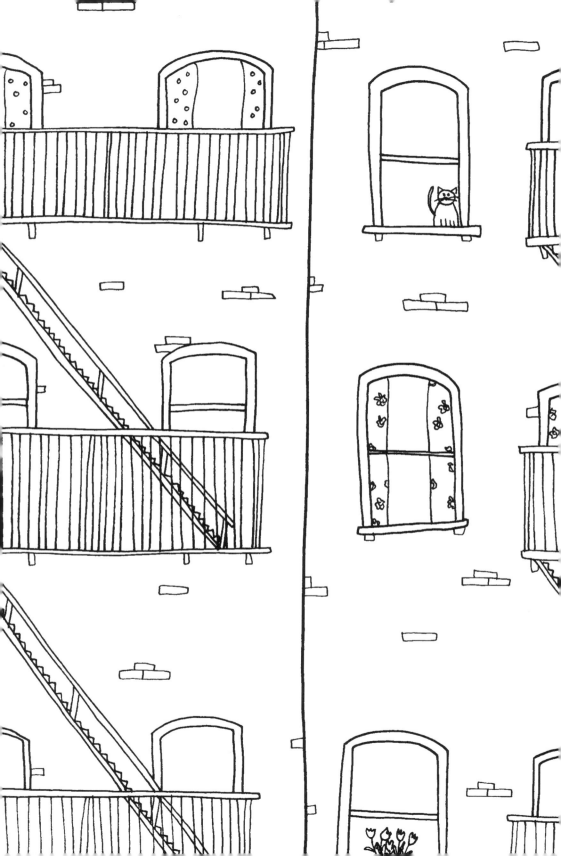

COME IN, WE'RE OPEN

You can shop in one of the large well-known department stores, or look for a nice concept store that also sells 'everything'.

4X DEPARTMENT STORE

☐ **BLOOMINGDALE'S**
   59th Street & Lexington Avenue
   New York City, NY 10022

☐ **SAKS FIFTH AVENUE**
   611 5th Avenue
   New York City, NY 10022

☐ **MACY'S HERALD SQUARE**
   151 West 34th Street
   New York City, NY 10001

☐ **BERGDORF GOODMAN**
   754 5th Avenue
   New York City, NY 10019

☐ ....

☐ ....

☐ ....

5X CONCEPT STORE

☐ **ASSEMBLY**
   170 Ludlow Street
   New York City, NY 10002

☐ **PROJECT NO.8**
   38 Orchard Street
   New York City, NY 10002

☐ **PERSONNEL OF NEW YORK**
   9 Greenwich Avenue
   New York City, NY 10014

☐ **ANTHROPOLOGIE**
   50 Rockefeller Center
   New York City, NY 10020

☐ **SATURDAYS SURF NYC**
   31 Crosby Street
   New York City, NY 10013

☐ ....

☐ ....

☐ ....

18 SUN GLASSES, BEARDS, BASEBALL CAPS & BEAUTIFUL HATS

GET CREATIVE!

Next time I'm in New York, then...

18-19 HOUSTON STREET / BOWERY WALL In 1982, Keith Haring made his first drawing here. This Popeye is by Crash (aka John Matos), but you will find a different mural each time.

30-31 BROOKLYN BRIDGE Connects Manhattan with Brooklyn.

64-65 FOUR FAMOUS HOTELS Of course, this street does not actually exist in reality. From left to right, these are the NoMad Hotel, SixtySoho, the Waldorf Astoria and the Whyte Hotel.

86-87 ABBREVIATIONS They love those in NYC. Tip of the veil: Dumbo = Down Under Manhattan Bridge, Tribeca = Triangle Below Canal Street, Noho = North of Houston Street, Soho = South of Houston Street, Nolita = North of Little Italy, and so forth!

100-101 WATER TANKS If you look up, you will not only see many high buildings, but all those water tanks as well. These are for storing drinking water, but also for water for the fire department.

120-121 RED BRICK BUILDINGS So beautiful, those old red brick buildings with their fire escapes along the facade. We just cannot get enough of them!

COLOPHON

ILLUSTRATIONS Anne van Haasteren
TEXT & COMPILATION Petra de Hamer
DESIGN Oranje Vormgevers

THIS IS MY NEW YORK
isbn 978-90-6369-420-3
2nd printing 2019

B/SPUBLISHERS

© Text by Petra de Hamer and illustrated by Anne van Haasteren
© English edition: BIS Publishers, Amsterdam, June 2016
© Original edition: Uitgeverij Mo'Media bv, Breda, The Netherlands, www.momedia.nl

This publication has been compiled with the utmost care. BIS Publishers cannot be held liable for any inadequacies in the text. Any comments can be addressed to: BIS Publishers, Building Het Sieraad, Postjesweg 1, 1057 DT Amsterdam. bis@bispublishers.com, www.bispublishers.com